Greek Culture

Rjurik Davidson

Series Editor **Rob Waring**

Level 6 - ⑥

Greek Culture

Rjurik Davidson

© 2017 Seed Learning, Inc.

Series Editor: Rob Waring
Acquisitions Editor: Liana Robinson
Copy Editor: Casey Malarcher
Cover/Interior Design: Andy Roh

ISBN: 978-1-9464-5255-9

10 9 8 7 6 5 4 3 2 1
21 20 19 18 17

Contents

Ancient Greece

Usually, many things about the world around us go unnoticed. Most of the time, we don't ask many questions about everyday things. For example, who designed our buildings? When was our system of government invented? Where do our stories and myths come from?

Greek columns

Interestingly, a lot of Western culture comes from the ancient Greeks (800–500 BC), who lived about 2,500 years ago! Greece is a country in southeastern Europe. At that time, it was a center of science, art, and culture.

Have you ever been to the theater? Do you think about science and nature? Do you live in a democratic society?

In each of these areas, the ancient Greeks developed important ideas that we still use today!

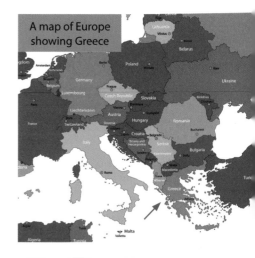

A map of Europe showing Greece

City-States

Ancient Greece wasn't actually a country 2,500 years ago. Rather, it was a group of city-states. Each city-state had its own government and army. Two of the most famous were called Athens and Sparta.

Athens, Greece

This was a glorious era in Greek history. The ancient Greeks were interested in everything! They built the best army in the world. They were pioneers in science, and they thought about how people could live better lives. They made some of the most beautiful art, and they wrote some of the greatest stories, especially about their gods and heroes.

Let's look at some of these amazing developments.

A Greek soldier

The Greek Army

Greek armor

The Greeks were very warlike and thought that all men should be able to fight. They fought with spears, swords, and shields. They wore armor and helmets. Can you imagine what war in ancient Greece was like? You would be able to see your enemy's eyes and hear their cries as you fought them hand to hand!

An image of the Greek phalanx

The Greeks developed some great military tactics. One tactic was called the phalanx. In the phalanx, the soldiers lined up together. They held long spears, with the front lines all pointing their spears to the front. Their enemies could not come close without being hurt.

The phalanx made the Greek army the most powerful in the world. They were able to defeat many of their enemies.

Soldiers fighting

A Slave Society

When the Greeks defeated their enemies, they made some of them into slaves. Ancient Greece was what we call a slave society. Their slaves were forced to work for the Greeks without pay. They had to do whatever the Greeks told them to do. The lives of slaves were full of hard work. They grew the plants, cooked the meals, and cleaned the houses.

A Greek woman and her slave

Owning slaves meant that the Greeks had a lot of spare time. This was one of the reasons they had time for other pursuits. They were able to organize a new type of government, think about how the world works, and make beautiful art.

A re-enactment of a slave market, where slaves were bought and sold

Sophia

Philomena

Chara

Eliss

Who Invented Democracy?

The Greeks thought a lot about the best kind of government. Was it best to live in a monarchy, where a king reigns and the people obey? The ancient Greeks who lived in Athens did not think so.

A politician argues for his ideas.

Instead, they invented what we call democracy. Democracy means "people power," and a democracy is when everyone can vote for their leaders. In Athens, only adult male citizens were allowed to vote. They met on a hill called the Pnyx two or three times a month.

The hill in Athens where the Greeks voted

During the meetings, the men would discuss many important issues and vote by a show of hands. Often, speakers debated and tried to convince the men in the crowd to vote in a particular way.

Voting by a show of hands

Philosophers and Scientists

When they weren't thinking about their government, many Greeks liked to think about the meaning of life. Why are we here? How do we live a happy life? How do we know if we are good people?

A Greek scientist

A philosopher is a person who asks these profound or deep questions. The word "philosophy" means the love of wisdom. There were many famous Greek philosophers like Aristotle and Plato. Many people still read their books.

Often, the Greek philosophers were also scientists. They developed a lot of the mathematics that we learn at school. They also invented the alarm clock, the odometer (which

A statue of the philosopher Socrates

is used to measure the distance a bicycle or car travels), and the science of map making. They discovered many things and were very innovative!

Socrates drinks poison after his trial.

Socrates was one of the most intelligent philosophers. He was also a bit peculiar. He wore the same clothes all year round. Plus, he liked walking around the city and asking people questions about their lives.

Socrates explains that he will always think about everything.

He would talk to anyone—young or old, slave or free, man or woman. Socrates asked them questions about everything!

In the year 399 BC, three Greeks accused Socrates of not worshipping the city's gods and of being a bad influence on young Greeks.

At his trial, Socrates refused to give up philosophy. The jury sentenced him to death, and he was forced to drink poison.

Socrates thinks about life.

Greek Stories

The Greeks were great at telling stories. In particular, they wrote famous poems and plays about their gods and heroes.

Modern actors in a Greek tragedy

Maybe you have seen or read a Greek tragedy in school. Famous Greek plays still performed today include *Medea* by Euripides, *Oedipus Rex* by Sophocles, and *Lysistrata* by Aristophanes.

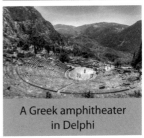

A Greek amphitheater in Delphi

The Greeks seemed to prefer plays that were tragedies over comedies. Greek tragedies were often about heroes who made terrible mistakes.

The plays were performed in beautiful outdoor theaters called amphitheaters. Many of these theaters still exist.

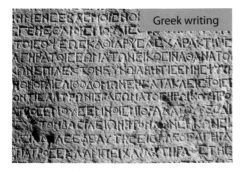

Greek writing

Another great writer from ancient Greece was Homer. He wrote long poems about Greek heroes: *The Iliad* and *The Odyssey*. They are still famous today!

Greek Gods and Heroes

The Greeks believed in many gods. There was the god of love, the god of hunting and war, the god of fire, and the god of the sea. These gods were always meddling in the lives of the Greeks and causing trouble!

The Cyclops, a one-eyed giant

The Greeks also had many legendary heroes and incredible monsters. These monsters

A mosaic of two Greek gods

included the Cyclops, which was a giant with only one eye. They also included the terrifying Hydra, which was a nine-headed water snake.

These myths are so interesting and imaginative that we still remember them today. Movies like *Hercules* and *Troy* feature brave heroes and terrifying monsters from ancient Greece.

A statue of Hercules fighting the Hydra

The Minotaur and Medusa

The Minotaur

Maybe you have heard of some famous Greek legends. One legend was the story of the Minotaur, a creature who was half-man and half-bull. One day, the queen of Crete gave birth to the Minotaur. The king was so horrified that he hid the Minotaur in a maze. Every year the king fed young men and women to the Minotaur.

One day, a brave hero called Theseus entered the maze. He tied the end of a ball of string to his starting place and kept the ball with him. As he searched the maze, he left a trail of string behind him. This was how he found his way out after he fought and killed the Minotaur.

A statue of the Minotaur

Theseus fighting the Minotaur

Perseus with the head of Medusa

Medusa

Another exciting legend is the story of Medusa. Medusa was one of three horrible sisters. They all had snakes instead of hair. If you looked into Medusa's eyes, she would turn you to stone. She was one of the scariest monsters!

The brave hero Perseus went to kill Medusa. To avoid looking at Medusa's eyes, he carried a shield. This shield was polished so that it looked like a mirror. Perseus looked into the shield instead of at Medusa herself. Finally, he saw Medusa and her sisters sleeping. Perseus crept up on Medusa quietly and cut off her head!

He then escaped from Medusa's sisters using a hat that made him invisible.

Greek Art

Greek pottery

Many of these myths are depicted in Greek art. The Greeks liked to paint their gods and heroes on pots. They also made sculptures of them.

What makes some art beautiful and some art ugly?

A Greek family

Many people think that Greek sculpture and pottery are some of the most beautiful ever made. Have a look at the sculptures and the pottery on this page. Are they beautiful? What do you think?

Greek art has influenced many artists throughout history. Lots of famous artists have painted scenes from Greek stories.

Statues which are also pillars

Beautiful Buildings

The remains of the Parthenon

The Greeks built many beautiful buildings. They invented their own style. They liked to include columns and intricate details.

The most famous Greek building is called the Parthenon. The remains of the Parthenon still stand on a hill in the center of the Greek city of Athens. Some people say that it was once the most magnificent building in the world. It is still quite beautiful.

Important buildings around the world often copy the Greek style. Many libraries, government buildings, and even homes use columns, for example.

Are there any buildings built in a classical Greek style in your hometown?

New York Public Library, built with Greek columns

A Part of Our Heritage

Ancient Greece is part of our heritage. We still tell ancient Greek stories and perform ancient Greek plays. We still study the science and philosophy that they left behind. We still copy their sculptures and buildings. Greek democracy lasted only two hundred years, but the idea returned thousands of years later. Most of us live in democratic countries today.

An ancient Greek statue

Perhaps now you will become more aware of the ancient Greek influneces in your everyday life.

A modern theater with a Greek influence

But what about our own time? What things do you think we might leave for the future? Which of our buildings will last? What cultural influences will be our legacy?

Comprehension Questions

1. What was ancient Greece?
   (a) A group of city-states
   (b) A god from a myth
   (c) A monarchy ruled by a king
   (d) One big democracy

2. What is a phalanx?
   (a) A group of brave citizens
   (b) A group of soldiers with swords
   (c) A Greek general
   (d) A military tactic that uses soldiers with spears

3. Greek slaves were...
   (a) usually from Greece.
   (b) treated like kings.
   (c) owned by Greeks.
   (d) allowed to vote.

4. A democracy is a society...
   (a) where everyone speaks on a hill to each other.
   (b) ruled by a king.
   (c) where people choose their leader.
   (d) where no one is hurt.

5. A philosopher is someone who...
   (a) builds detailed buildings.
   (b) lives very simply.
   (c) makes people uncomfortable.
   (d) asks profound questions about life.

6. Socrates was accused of...
   (a) not worshipping the gods and of being a bad influence.
   (b) being a bad writer.
   (c) wearing the same clothes every day.
   (d) asking too many questions.

7. What is a Greek tragedy?
   (a) A sad thing that happens in life
   (b) A mistake that many people make
   (c) A very sad play
   (d) A person who is very sad

8. How did Theseus find his way out of the maze?
   (a) By using a map
   (b) By using a ball of string
   (c) By using his shield
   (d) By asking the Minotaur

9. What happened when someone looked into Medusa's eyes?
   (a) The person ran away.
   (b) The person fell asleep.
   (c) The person screamed.
   (d) The person turned to stone.

10. Where is the Parthenon?
   (a) On a hill in the center of Athens
   (b) In New York
   (c) Lost somewhere in Greece
   (d) In Paris

Key 1. (a) 2. (d) 3. (c) 4. (c) 5. (d) 6. (a) 7. (c) 8. (b) 9. (d) 10. (a)

18

Glossary

- **amphitheater** a large area with seats rising in curved rows around an open space
- **convince** to persuade someone or make them believe something
- **depict** to represent something by using a picture or words
- **heritage** something that is handed down from the past
- **innovative** using ideas that are new
- **intricate** having a lot of details
- **legacy** something that remains from an earlier time
- **magnificent** very beautiful or impressive; very great
- **maze** a complex system of passages
- **peculiar** unusual and strange
- **pioneer** a person who is one of the first people to do something
- **pottery** objects that are made out of clay and then baked at high temperatures
- **pursuit** an activity that a person spends time doing, usually when not working
- **reign** to rule a country, like a king or emperor
- **terrifying** very scary; causing great fear
- **tragedy** a play about death or suffering with a sad ending
- **worship** to have or show respect for a god or gods

Image Credit/Pages

World History
Timeline

This chart shows a rough overview of world history.
Some of the dates have been simplified.

World History Timeline

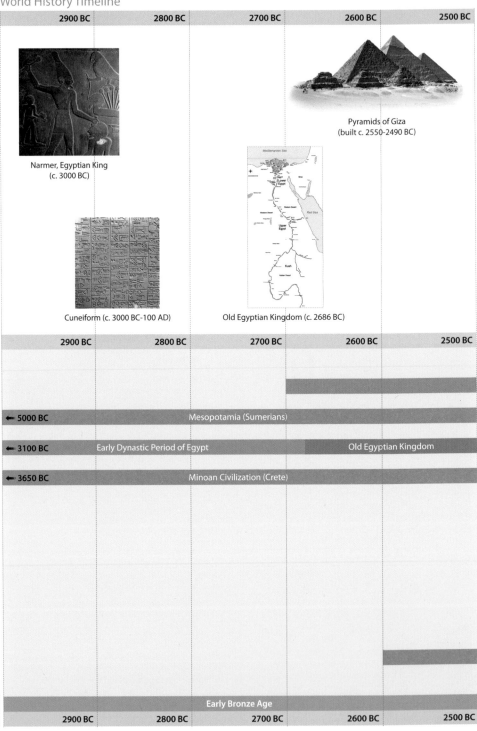

	2900 BC	2800 BC	2700 BC	2600 BC	2500 BC

Narmer, Egyptian King
(c. 3000 BC)

Pyramids of Giza
(built c. 2550-2490 BC)

Cuneiform (c. 3000 BC-100 AD)

Old Egyptian Kingdom (c. 2686 BC)

	2900 BC	2800 BC	2700 BC	2600 BC	2500 BC

◀ 5000 BC Mesopotamia (Sumerians)

◀ 3100 BC Early Dynastic Period of Egypt · Old Egyptian Kingdom

◀ 3650 BC Minoan Civilization (Crete)

Early Bronze Age

	2900 BC	2800 BC	2700 BC	2600 BC	2500 BC

2400 BC	2300 BC	2200 BC	2100 BC	2000 BC

Gudea of Lagash
(c. 2144-2124 BC)

Sahure, Egyptian King
(c. 2487-2475 BC)

Sargon the Great,
Akkadian King
(c. 2340-2284 BC)

Indus Valley
Civilization

Ur III Dynasty (c. 2112-2004 BC)

2400 BC	2300 BC	2200 BC	2100 BC	2000 BC

Xia Dynasty

Gutian Dynasty

Elam (Iran)

Akkadian Empire

Ur III Dynasty

Assyria (Early Period)

Middle Egyptian Kingdom

Minoan Civilization (Crete)

1st Intermediate
Period

Indus Valley Civilization (India)

2400 BC	2300 BC	2200 BC	2100 BC	2000 BC

World History Timeline

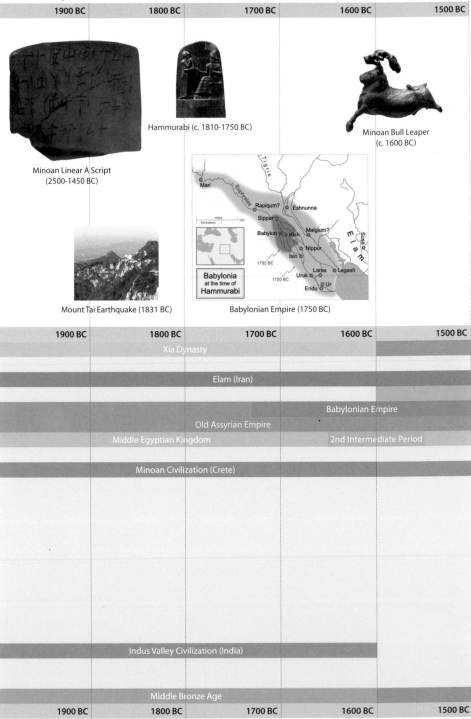

| 1900 BC | 1800 BC | 1700 BC | 1600 BC | 1500 BC |

Minoan Linear A Script
(2500-1450 BC)

Hammurabi (c. 1810-1750 BC)

Minoan Bull Leaper
(c. 1600 BC)

Mount Tai Earthquake (1831 BC)

Babylonian Empire (1750 BC)

Mari
Rapiqum?   Eshnunna
Sippar
Babylon   Kish   Malgium?
Nippur
Isin
1792 BC   Larsa   Lagash
1750 BC   Uruk   Ur
Eridu

Babylonia
at the time of
Hammurabi

Elam

| 1900 BC | 1800 BC | 1700 BC | 1600 BC | 1500 BC |

Xia Dynasty

Elam (Iran)

Babylonian Empire

Old Assyrian Empire

Middle Egyptian Kingdom

2nd Intermediate Period

Minoan Civilization (Crete)

Indus Valley Civilization (India)

Middle Bronze Age

| 1900 BC | 1800 BC | 1700 BC | 1600 BC | 1500 BC |

World History Timeline

1400 BC	1300 BC	1200 BC	1100 BC	1000 BC

Moses (c. 1391-1271 BC)

Homer

Shang Oracle Bone

Tutankhamun
(ruled c. 1332-1323 BC)

Battle of Kadesh (1274 BC)

Phoenician Alphabet
(c. 1200-150 BC)

1400 BC	1300 BC	1200 BC	1100 BC	1000 BC

Shang Dynasty

Elam (Iran)

Hittites — Neo-Hittites

Middle Assyrian Empire

New Egyptian Kingdom

Mycenaean Greece — Greek Dark Ages

Phoenicia

Olmec Civilization (Mexico)

Vedic Period in India

Late Bronze Age — Early Iron Age

1400 BC	1300 BC	1200 BC	1100 BC	1000 BC

World History Timeline

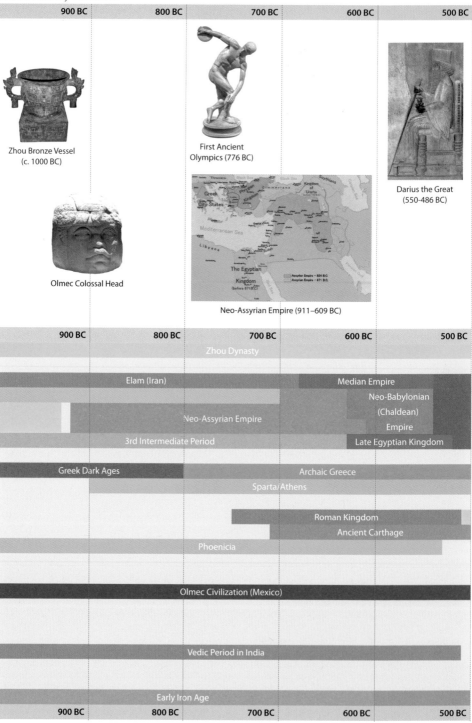

900 BC	800 BC	700 BC	600 BC	500 BC

Zhou Bronze Vessel (c. 1000 BC)

First Ancient Olympics (776 BC)

Olmec Colossal Head

Neo-Assyrian Empire (911–609 BC)

Darius the Great (550-486 BC)

900 BC	800 BC	700 BC	600 BC	500 BC

Zhou Dynasty

Elam (Iran)

Median Empire

Neo-Babylonian (Chaldean) Empire

Neo-Assyrian Empire

3rd Intermediate Period

Late Egyptian Kingdom

Greek Dark Ages

Archaic Greece

Sparta/Athens

Roman Kingdom

Ancient Carthage

Phoenicia

Olmec Civilization (Mexico)

Vedic Period in India

Early Iron Age

900 BC	800 BC	700 BC	600 BC	500 BC

400 BC	300 BC	200 BC	100 BC	0

Alexander the Great
(356-323 BC)

Hannibal
(247-183 BC)

Julius Caesar
(100-44 BC)

Cleopatra
(69-30 BC)

Battle of Salamis
(480 BC)

Seleucid Empire (312-63 BC)

Rossetta Stone
(created 196 BC)

400 BC	300 BC	200 BC	100 BC	0

Zhou Dynasty

Qin

Han Dynasty

Achaemenid (Persian) Empire

Alexander the Great

Parthian Empire

Seleucid Empire
Ptolemaic Kingdom
(Hellenistic Greece)

Classical Greece

Sparta/Athens

Roman Empire

Roman Republic

Roman Empire

Maurya Empire

Middle Iron Age

400 BC	300 BC	200 BC	100 BC	0

World History Timeline

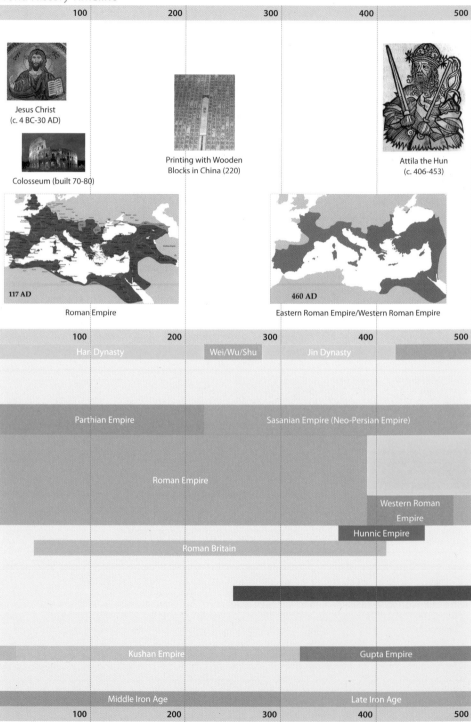

| 100 | 200 | 300 | 400 | 500 |

Jesus Christ
(c. 4 BC-30 AD)

Colosseum (built 70-80)

Printing with Wooden
Blocks in China (220)

Attila the Hun
(c. 406-453)

117 AD

Roman Empire

460 AD

Eastern Roman Empire/Western Roman Empire

| 100 | 200 | 300 | 400 | 500 |

Han Dynasty

Wei/Wu/Shu

Jin Dynasty

Parthian Empire

Sasanian Empire (Neo-Persian Empire)

Roman Empire

Western Roman
Empire

Hunnic Empire

Roman Britain

Kushan Empire

Gupta Empire

Middle Iron Age

Late Iron Age

| 100 | 200 | 300 | 400 | 500 |

World History Timeline

Pope Gregory I
(c. 540-604)

Charlemagne
(742-814)

Vikings Discover
America (1000)

Muhammad (c. 570-632)

Umayyad Caliphate (661-750)

Holy Roman Empire (800-1806)

Tang Dynasty

Liao Dynasty

Northern &
Southern Dynasties

Sui Dynasty

5 Dynasties and
10 Kingdoms

Rashidun
Caliphate

Umayyad
Caliphate

Abbasid Caliphate

Eastern Roman (Byzantine) Empire

Francia

West Francia

East Francia

Anglo-Saxon Kingdoms

Viking Age

Mayan Empire

Gurjara-Pratihara Dynasty

Early Middle Age

World History Timeline

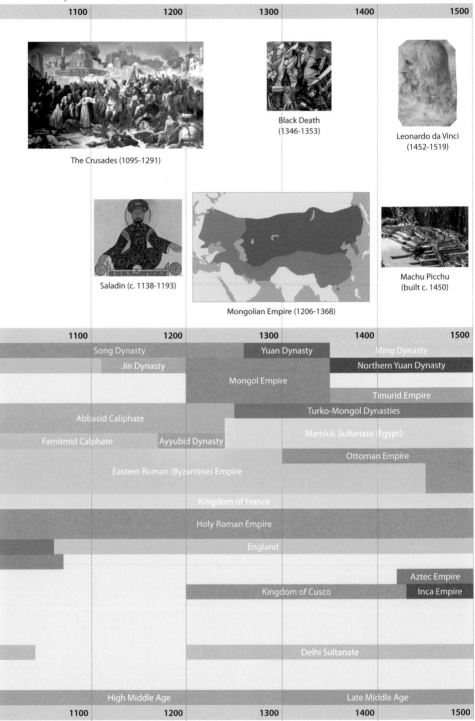

The Crusades (1095-1291)

Black Death (1346-1353)

Leonardo da Vinci (1452-1519)

Saladin (c. 1138-1193)

Mongolian Empire (1206-1368)

Machu Picchu (built c. 1450)

| 1100 | 1200 | 1300 | 1400 | 1500 |

Song Dynasty
Yuan Dynasty
Ming Dynasty

Jin Dynasty
Northern Yuan Dynasty

Mongol Empire

Timurid Empire

Abbasid Caliphate
Turko-Mongol Dynasties

Famitmid Calphate
Ayyubid Dynasty
Mamluk Sultanate (Egypt)

Ottoman Empire

Eastern Roman (Byzantine) Empire

Kingdom of France

Holy Roman Empire

England

Aztec Empire
Inca Empire
Kingdom of Cusco

Delhi Sultanate

High Middle Age
Late Middle Age

| 1100 | 1200 | 1300 | 1400 | 1500 |

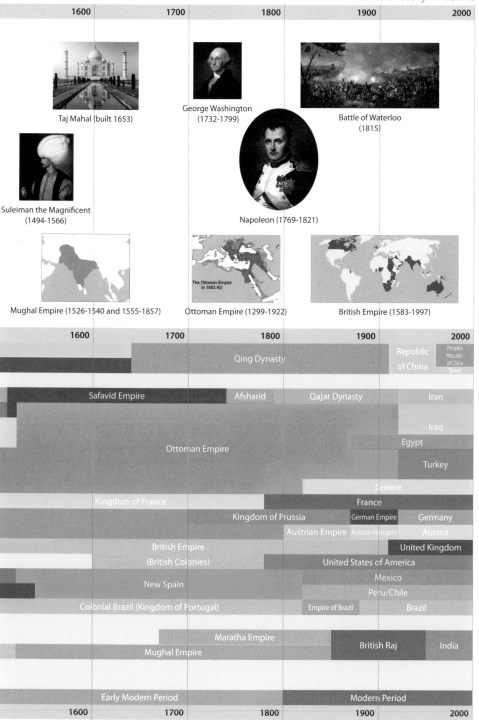

World History Timeline

Taj Mahal (built 1653)

George Washington (1732-1799)

Battle of Waterloo (1815)

Suleiman the Magnificent (1494-1566)

Napoleon (1769-1821)

Mughal Empire (1526-1540 and 1555-1857)

The Ottoman Empire in 1683 AD

Ottoman Empire (1299-1922)

British Empire (1583-1997)

Qing Dynasty

Republic of China

People's Republic of China Taiwan

Safavid Empire

Afsharid

Qajar Dynasty

Iran

Iraq

Ottoman Empire

Egypt

Turkey

Greece

Kingdom of France

France

Kingdom of Prussia

German Empire

Germany

Austrian Empire

Austria-Hungary

Austria

British Empire

(British Colonies)

United Kingdom

United States of America

New Spain

Mexico

Peru/Chile

Colonial Brazil (Kingdom of Portugal)

Empire of Brazil

Brazil

Maratha Empire

British Raj

India

Mughal Empire

Early Modern Period

Modern Period

List of Books